WRITE THAT(A⁺) ESSAY!

HIGH SCHOOL EDITION

For the writer in you:
that you might succeed at essay writing—
and even enjoy doing it!

Ian Hunter, 2011

About the author:

Dr Ian Hunter, Ph.D. is an Associate Professor at The University of Auckland Business School. A best-selling author and educator, Ian writes on creativity, innovation, history, education, and business. He is a frequent conference speaker and media commentator. He lives in Auckland, New Zealand, with his wife Debra and their five children.

WRITE THAT (A⁺) ESSAY!

HIGH SCHOOL EDITION

The outrageously helpful guide
to writing better essays and
achieving higher grades

Dr Ian Hunter Ph.D.

Designed by Sharon Grace

Printed in China by Prolong Press Ltd

Hunter Publishing

PO Box 24687

Royal Oak

Auckland 1345

ISBN: 978-0-9876558-0-6

A catalogue record for this book is available from the National Library of New Zealand.

www.writethatessay.org

CONTENTS

Planning Techniques

Writing an Introduction

The Body Paragraph

Writing Conclusions

Writing Better Sentences

Polishing Your Work: Techniques to Make Your Essay Shine

Essay-Writing Readiness Test

Before you start reading this book, take 20 seconds to complete this helpful little test.
(Circle the option that best reflects you).

When asked to write an essay do you:

a) Happily write the essay
b) Sit down at your desk and look out the window
c) Go to footie practice instead
d) Ask your little brother or sister to write the essay
e) Pay your big brother or sister to write the essay
f) Suffer from dizzy spells
g) Search the net for sign-up details for the French Foreign Legion
h) Have a sudden onset of not-able-to-go-to-school syndrome
i) Email your local MP demanding a review of old-fashioned teaching methods
j) Mutter 'essays are for losers' in your sleep
k) Search the internet for schools that don't write essays
l) Hunt the web for essays already written . . .?

If you selected a), shame on you. If you selected any other option, you are in the right place.
By reading this book you will find out that you can succeed at essay writing, get the grades you have been hoping for, and still have time for footie practice!

Happy reading!

Welcome

If you find writing school essays difficult, congratulations, you are in the right place! Many students do. Let's face it: if you could do absolutely anything else on the whole planet, apart from write an essay, you would (with the possible exception of eating Brussels sprouts or doing statistics homework).

What is it that makes writing essays so difficult? One of the key reasons is that no one sits you down and explains to you the rules of essay writing. You need to know what is expected of you when you write an essay, and how to write a great school essay. In this short book, I show you how to do just that.

It's important that you excel at essay writing. Because it doesn't matter if you end up studying to be a nurse, an engineer, a vicar, a veterinarian, an airline pilot, a lawyer, a gym manager, or a computer programmer. At some point your ability will be tested by your skill at writing essays.

To succeed, you need to know how to express yourself accurately and well with words. Writing essays does this. It teaches you to order your thinking, demonstrates that you can analyse your ideas, and shows that you can convince someone else of the merits of a situation.

As you master essay writing and begin to write more confidently, your grades will start to reflect the kinds of talents that you really do possess. Because after helping thousands of students with their essay writing at all sorts of levels, I know that you have real writing talents lurking inside that are just waiting to emerge.

Time to get on with it!

Happy writing,
Ian Hunter

ESSAY WRITING

Essay Writing and Cricket

Thoughts from a sports lover:

Essay writing is a bit like the sport of cricket. Say, you dislike cricket. However, one afternoon, one of the school's top cricket coaches shows you how to hold the bat properly. Then he demonstrates how your poor stance at the crease was making it easy for the bowlers to get you out.

A week later, the team captain spends a couple of hours with you on your bowling. He shows you that how you hold your head influences where the ball travels as it leaves your hand. With some practice, all of a sudden those deliveries of yours that were veering towards the outfield are now flying straight towards the wickets of the opposing players. You bowl someone out. You start to hit a few runs, knock a great four in your second match, and all of a sudden, you are standing on the pitch one Saturday morning, thinking: 'I really like this game!'

How did this transformation take place? The game hasn't altered. Cricket is still cricket, and possibly quite boring to some people. What has changed is that your increase in skill has altered your attitude toward the sport. Your previous fears have subsided, and you have a new confidence and expectation in your ability. All this happened because someone took the time to show you the basic skills of the game.

Writing is the same.

It is unrealistic to think that you are going to pick up your pen and words will miraculously flow on the page like Charles Dickens or Ernest Hemingway. However, it is **totally realistic** to think that with a bit more knowledge and practice you will start to write with more confidence and more flair than you ever did before.

> Master the essay. Impress your teachers. Get higher grades. You can do it!

I say all this because, as you enter your high school years, you need to master the art of essay writing. I'm sure you would much rather be assessed on your drawing ability, or your charm, or your sense of humour. All these are important. But, in the final exam, that teacher who has been so good to you all year is going to want you to write an essay to see if you learned anything. Follow the advice in this book and you will blow their socks off. Master the essay. Impress your teachers. Get higher grades. You can do it!

What's an Essay?

The place to start is to understand what an essay actually is. And just as importantly, it is helpful to understand what an essay is not. An essay is not a narrative, it is not a description of events, it is not a careful retelling of a story, it is not a splurge of ideas as they come pouring out of your head.

An ESSAY is an ARGUMENT.

This does not mean that you are standing on your desk waving your fist at everyone as you recite your work. An essay is an argument because the purpose of an essay is to take a position on a question, and then argue your viewpoint based on evidence.

To do this well means you need to decide what your point of view is, you need to spend some time gathering good examples and information to argue your essay, and you need to consider your ideas carefully as you write them. Add some polish with thoughtful and interesting sentences and you have the makings of a top-class piece of work.

Essays Have a Clear Structure

One of the things that it is helpful to understand about essay writing from the outset is that essay writing has an accepted form and structure. It is expected, for example, that your essay will have an introduction, a body, and a conclusion. There are also expected lengths for these sections, which provide the foundations of a well-written essay.

For example, a good essay writer doesn't overwrite the introduction. In fact, you don't need to spend long on the introduction at all—its purpose is to get your essay under way and to tell the person reading the essay what your overall argument is. The real marks are gained from what you write in the body of your essay.

In the body of your essay you use analysis. And you do this whether you are discussing poetry, or art, or economics, or Shakespeare: they are all handled with the same basic techniques, as you scrutinise and discuss the points you are making.

Does this sound more interesting than just lamely writing out what you think the teacher wants to hear? It should. Because it is. Once you know what is expected of you, you can really start to enjoy the cut and thrust of putting forward your ideas strongly.

Summary

An essay is: an argument based on evidence, clearly structured, and grounded in analysis.

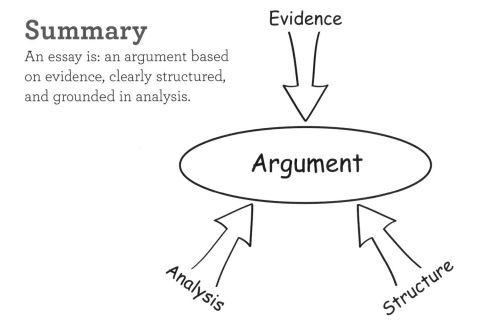

More Than One Plausible Answer

Unlike maths, an essay question can have several plausible answers. That means that for precisely the same essay question, you could compose an answer boldly arguing one side of the question and get an A. Your friend, sitting right next to you in class, could answer the same question from a different point of view and also receive an A grade.

Once you know what is expected of you, you can really start to enjoy the cut and thrust of putting forward your ideas strongly.

The reason for this is that in essay writing, teachers are looking for HOW WELL you assemble your case—how convincing your argument is—and the quality of evidence that you submit.

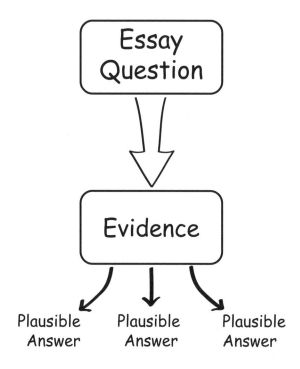

Essay Question

Evidence

Plausible Answer   Plausible Answer   Plausible Answer

Expand Your Knowledge

Writing a good essay demands broadening your knowledge. The ideas that you presently have in your head about a topic can be a good start. But they are only a beginning. In the same way that you learn new things in class, your teacher is expecting that the better essay writers will push further than just what is discussed in class and find new and additional information for their essays.

This doesn't mean that you need to spend weeks tracking down evidence. It does mean, however, that doing some basic research will give you more to discuss in your essay and improve the quality of your answer. Here are a few suggestions to get you started gathering information for your essay.

Research for Essays

It might surprise you, but it's better NOT to go online first to find research material for your essays. School and community libraries are an excellent source of information, and can provide trustworthy material.

★ Spend an afternoon in your local library seeing what you can uncover on your topic. Ask the librarian for assistance.

★ Read an encyclopedia entry on your topic—that's often a good place to begin.

★ If you are studying a poem or book, find a biography about your author or poet and read that.

★ Read a biography about a historical figure you are studying. A biography can help you understand someone's motives and the context in which they lived.

★ Look at the end of book chapters for a reference list (or in the bibliography) to see what other books or articles have been written on your topic. Go and find some of these, as someone else has already done the hard work for you, isolating what is useful material.

★ Every subject that you study has specialist professional publications dedicated to it, such as historical or literary magazines, even engineering and design magazines. These can be a useful source of mini case studies for your essay, and can inspire your writing in new directions.

★ Don't forget newspaper articles: newspapers contain some fantastic reviews on books, as well as important historical or economic information. Searching these online can be a helpful thing to do.

★ Take notes while you do your research. Don't leave it till the end. One useful technique is to start a fresh page for each new book or article from which you gather material. When you finish your research, you can stick the pages on your wall, or lay them out on a desk, and begin to collate your thoughts about what to write.

The point of doing research is to add to the knowledge already in your head. In the process, you will discover new ways of thinking about the question you have been asked for your essay. And, you will find more interesting evidence from which to construct your argument.

The Courtroom

Another way to think about writing essays is to consider a courtroom. Hopefully, you will never see the inside of a courtroom from the dock, but use your imagination for a moment, think about that point where the judge and jury sit down and the defence counsel stands up to make their opening statement.

Would you want your lawyer to stand up and say: 'Good morning, Your Honour. Your Honour, my client here may be guilty of this heinous crime, or, on the other hand, he may not be guilty. Either is possible.'

Who would want a lawyer like that! No one. You want a lawyer who is going to stand up and yell: 'Mr Brown is NOT guilty Your Honour, and I am going to show you why today, with absolutely convincing evidence!'

Make a Case

Essay writing is just the same as that courtroom. Like a good lawyer, your teacher is expecting that you won't just sit there and be neutral, but that you will adopt a position on your question. You may argue one side or the other—but he or she expects you to take a stand and make a case. And again like a good lawyer, your teacher is expecting that you will present some robust evidence to back up your case, not just say the first thing that pops into your head.

> Like a good lawyer, your teacher is expecting that you will present some robust evidence to back up your case.

Not a Detective Story

An essay is not like your favourite detective story. A detective story keeps you in page-turning suspense. It isn't until the final moment that you find out that the crime was committed by Professor Plum, in the conservatory, with the candlestick! (I knew he was rotten to the core...)

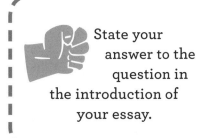

State your answer to the question in the introduction of your essay.

But some people do treat essay writing just like being a successful crime writer. They think that their job is to hold back their great 'Aha!' moment until the very end of the essay, carefully keeping the reader in spine-tingling suspense before finally revealing their big CONCLUSION.

Sorry to disappoint you. But in a word: WRONG. The convention in essay writing is that you state your big 'Aha!' right up front, in your introduction. Make it clear and firm! It's one of the rules of essay composition.

Be an Essay Writer, Not a Novelist

State your case firmly, clearly, and boldly in the opening paragraph of your essay. Then, in the body of your essay demonstrate why this point of view is so important. That's what the BEST essay writers do.

Sections of an Essay

An essay has three sections: the **introduction**, the **body**, and the **conclusion**. When it comes time to write your essay, you need to know how much to write for your essay overall, and how many words to write for each section of the essay.

The following table tells you how much you need to write for differing lengths of essay. This is based on the fact that most students write about 280–300 words per side of an A4 piece of paper (which is about 8–10 words per line). Have a look below, and see how much you need to write.

Essay Length

If you are asked to write a:
400-word essay—that is basically a page and a half
500-word essay—that is a page and two thirds
600-word essay—that is two pages
800-word essay—that is two and a half pages
5000-word essay—it's time for university.

In the following section, I break down these overall essay lengths into more specific components, showing you how much you are expected to write for your introduction, your body, and your conclusion. These are a guide only, but they provide a helpful starting place.

Think in Paragraphs

One of the keys to good essay writing is to think in paragraphs. A paragraph is a collection of sentences exploring a single idea, and paragraphs are the building blocks of essay construction. At high school, the paragraphs you write should be, on average, 80–100 words long. That is 4 or 5 good-sized sentences per paragraph.

 At high school, the paragraphs you write should be, on average, 80–100 words long. That is 4 or 5 good-sized sentences per paragraph.

NOW, time for a formula for those of you who like maths. How do you figure out how much to write for your essay? If you have to write 400 words for an essay, first of all you subtract the introduction (allow 60 words for your introduction: 3 sentences of 20 words per sentence). Then, subtract the conclusion (allow 80 words for your conclusion: 4 good-sized sentences). That means you have 260 words left for the body of your essay: 260 words is 3 short paragraphs of 86 words each—that's only 4.5 sentences per paragraph. You can do that.

Always think in terms of how many paragraphs you have to write to complete your essay. This will also then tell you how many points you need to assemble for your evidence as you will be exploring one point per paragraph.

Words Per Essay Section

Here is the number of words you can allow for each of the essay lengths I gave you before (see page 22). For each of them, I now also give you the number of paragraphs you would be expected to write in the body section of the essay.

A handy table

Occasionally, you might write a paragraph that has 6 sentences in it, instead of 4 or 5. That's fine. But anything shorter than 80 words starts not to look like a paragraph any more in English. At high school level, paragraphs longer than 120 words begins to look like you are writing a book, not an essay. So use this handy table as a guide to planning your work.

Remember: **think in paragraphs**. When you get your essay question from your teacher, look at the number of words required, and then think: 'Okay, that means I need to write 4 paragraphs for the body of my essay.' And immediately, you can start to think about what you will put in each of those 4 paragraphs. See how this concentrates your thinking?

	Introduction	Body	Conclusion
400-word essay	60 words (3 sentences)	260 words (3 short paragraphs)	80 words (4 sentences)
500-word essay	60 words (3 sentences)	340 words (4 paragraphs)	100 words (5 sentences)
600-word essay	60 words (3 sentences)	440 words (5 paragraphs)	100 words (5 sentences)
800-word essay	60 words (3 sentences)	640 words (6 paragraphs)	100 words (5 sentences)

STRATEGIES
TO GET YOU
STARTED

Getting Started

The biggest difficulty people face when writing an essay is starting. Your mind locks up. You sit staring blankly at the page, and cannot think of the first thing to say. If you feel like this, even in a small way, relax. You are not alone.

GOOD NEWS: this problem is easily fixed. In fact, you are going to be completely rid of this problem very quickly, AND, you will never suffer from it ever again.

> Your first sentence does not need to be brilliant—you just need to get things going.

But before I give you some sure-fire solutions to the starting problem, there are THREE things you need to realise:

a) You do not need a brilliant first sentence to write an A-grade essay. That's right: your first sentence does not need to be brilliant—you just need to get things going.
b) If you are not a creative type, a neutral sentence will ALWAYS work as a great first sentence in an essay (I will teach you how to write one of these shortly—they are VERY easy).
c) The biggest cause of first-sentence freeze is 'Introduction Ignorance'. What's this? A complete lack of knowledge about what an introduction needs to ACHIEVE in an essay. Once you know this, you are away.

What follows are 10 practical strategies that will help you overcome your essay-starting worries. Find the one that works for you, and go for it.

10 Sure-Fire Strategies to Get You Writing Faster

Strategy 1: Make a Hit List

One of the problems with getting your essay started is that you can sit in a motionless state for too long with lots of ideas floating round your mind. You could be thinking: 'Oh, I could write about this, I could discuss that, I must mention this in my essay.' Or: 'I wonder what's for dinner?'

The end result of all this musing is that you sit there for 15 minutes or more and nothing gets written. You stare forlornly down at your blank paper, see there is nothing written, and decide that essay writing is difficult, and resolve to do some more thinking. While I agree that it is enjoyable just to let your thoughts wander, this approach is a disaster.

Try a hit list to snap you out of it:

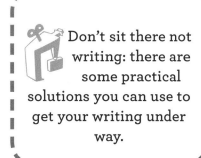

Don't sit there not writing: there are some practical solutions you can use to get your writing under way.

Step one

Grab a pen and just empty out on paper all the things that you know about this subject. Everything that comes to mind. As they pop up, write them down in a list. At this point, two things will happen: one, you will start, as you begin to write, to think of more things about your topic that had not occurred to you before—this is good; two, your blank piece of paper now has some writing on it—you have started your essay!

Step two

Once you have your list in front of you, take your pen and draw a circle around any of the key ideas that you think might be good to write about for your essay. If you get three or four circles, you have a basic essay plan with each circle representing one paragraph in your essay. You are away.

Strategy 2: The 'Brilliant First Time' Complex

Some people get frozen at the start of their essay by the 'Brilliant First Time' complex. Somebody told them, or they just thought it up themselves one day, that really good writers pick up their pen and the words just flow awesomely first time. And if they aren't like this too, then they must be a hopeless writer. What a load of nonsense!

Let me offer you some encouragement from the story of a great author, Roald Dahl, who wrote *Charlie and the Chocolate Factory*, and many other superb stories. Roald was a typical writer. He knew that good writing did not come out the first time he wrote, but that doing a draft was part of the process toward achieving the finished article.

Charlie and the Chocolate Factory actually started life as a book called *Charlie's Chocolate Boy*. In this draft there were ten children in the story. Then, Roald redrafted the book, and the number of children was reduced to seven; then he did it again with six kids; then, finally, did it again with five children. And those magnificent little worker creatures in Willy Wonka's chocolate factory: they had their name changed from Whipple-Scrumpets to Oompa-Loompas! And all this over the course of three years and multiple drafts.

Am I telling you that your essay is going to take three years to write? No. What I am telling you is that good writers produce drafts. No one writes golden letters straight from the pen. So stop thinking that you should also. Pick up your pen, have a go, and produce the first draft. If you are a good writer, you will then follow that with another draft. (For more on this technique, see page 98).

Strategy 3: Read Some More

If you are stuck not knowing what to say, often you just haven't read enough about your topic yet. This is more common than you think. Don't expect too much from yourself early on: read some more books, articles, reports, or speeches on your topic. You will discover fresh perspectives and information that had not occurred to you previously. Soon, your challenge will be what to **leave out** of your essay, not what to **put in**.

Strategy 4: Make a Sandwich

If you are really stuck for inspiration, take five minutes, go to the kitchen, open the refrigerator and make a sandwich. This won't help your writing one little bit, but you will enjoy eating the sandwich, which is better than sitting there feeling miserable for yourself not writing anything. Then, come back to the desk and start to plan your essay.

Strategy 5: Go For a Run

Now, this is not as silly as it sounds. Some of you are just far too stressed about the whole idea of writing. You need to lower your anxiety so you feel better about life, and certainly better about the idea of writing this essay. Physical exercise reduces your stress levels. In fact, 20 minutes of physical exercise will reduce your stress levels by 25 per cent. So, grab your jogging shoes from wherever you've hidden them, get outside in the fresh air, and go for a run or a walk. It will clear your head. When you come home, it will be easier to write. And you will be fitter. That's a bonus.

Strategy 6: Mind Maps

A mind map is easy to create. Take a large sheet of paper (I always need space to think) and in the centre write a single word or the topic for your essay. Then, on lines coming out from this single word, write other words as they come to mind that are connected to the topic. As you write words on these outer reaches of the diagram, you can extend these lines also, so that you end up with a lovely spidery diagram like the one below.

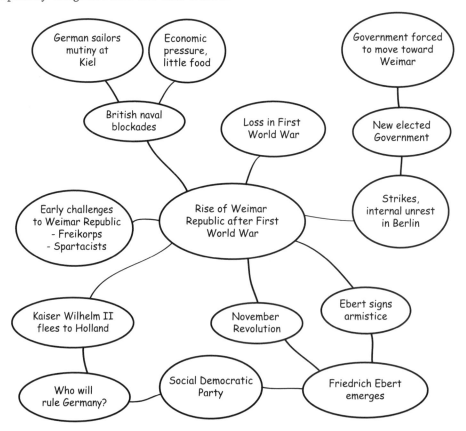

The real strength of the mind map is that it allows you to empty out all the ideas that are racing round your brain and capture them on a single page. Holding too many thoughts in your head at once can bring confusion and hold you back from starting your essay. The other benefit of mind-mapping is that it allows you to visualise the problem or the essay you have to write as a single picture, and see the main areas that you would like to explore.

Remember, ideas are not passive. Solutions come more quickly when we are doing something. So, if being stuck for ideas to start your essay describes you, take action. All the suggestions made here are active. Pick one and have a go. Taking action will help break the inactivity cycle and you will feel more encouraged and excited as you start to move forward.

Strategy 7: Speak a List

Do you feel better talking about things than writing them down on a piece of paper? Good. Why don't you use that skill to help you with your essay writing? Try speaking out loud a list of all the words that spring to mind about a particular topic. As you speak them out, write them down.

> If you are a person who likes to think out loud, try speaking your essay—it works.

Do this for about five minutes. Then, stop and have a look at your list of words. Now you have some ideas on this topic, because the speaking out has helped to break through the barriers that held you back inside.

Strategy 8: Tell Someone Else

This one also works especially well if you are someone who likes to think out loud. Sitting in silence can be the worst thing for you. So, grab someone sitting close—a brother or sister, a parent—and say: 'Hey, can I just explain something to you? I just want to get my ideas out.'

Do this and you will find that fresh connections snap together in your mind because the 'talking out loud' generates momentum for new ideas. You will have more options to consider when it comes to planning your essay.

Strategy 9: Cross-examine Your Question

Stuck for ideas? Try having a second look at your question. Now, start taking it apart piece by piece. Do a little mental dissection. Are you sure that you understand what each word in your question means? If not, grab a dictionary and check. Do you understand what the question is asking you to do? Try rephrasing the question in your own words. Say it out loud: 'SO, this question is asking me to . . .'

Sometimes, you can be stuck for ideas because you haven't thought through the question enough yet. Thinking about it in more detail can give you a breakthrough.

> Make sure you have read the question— several times if necessary. Ensure you understand what it is asking you to do.

Strategy 10: The Storyboard

Here's a variation on the mind map idea. Think of your essay as a storyboard. Filmmakers use storyboards to construct how a movie plays out. Each storyboard contains a small picture of what is occurring at that point in the movie, and a description of the scene that is taking place—perhaps with some key dialogue.

You can use a similar technique for your essay. Grab some 3in x

5in cards or 6in x 4in cards. On each card, sketch a key element of the essay that you want to discuss—just do a simple sketch drawing, nothing too elaborate. Around the drawing you might list some key facts or figures (or a useful quote) that you would like to incorporate when you discuss the point your picture represents. Check out the example below:

Origins of the First World War

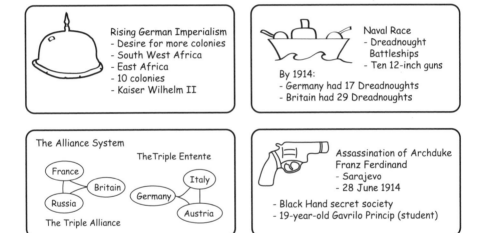

Do ONE storyboard card for each point that you think you might like to discuss in your essay. When you have finished drawing your storyboard cards, lay them out on the desk in front of you. Looking at the cards, select the one that you think you would like to discuss first in your essay. Then pick up the second card you would like to discuss. Carry on like this until you have all the cards in your hands that seem relevant to your essay.

You have just completed two VITAL STEPS to writing a great essay. You have creatively drawn up the key points you want to mention in your essay AND you have selected the best order in which to discuss those points. You are now ready to begin writing your essay, and can do so from the cards in your hand.

UNDERSTANDING
QUESTIONS

You and Questions

Knowing What to Write

Part of writing a good essay is becoming familiar with the sorts of questions you might get asked, and knowing what's expected of you in answering those questions.

While we can't cover all the possible variations of questions you might get asked, there are some very common forms of questions that teachers (and examiners) use. Understand them, and you really help yourself out when it comes to writing essays. Here's SEVEN of the more common ones to get you started:

1. Pure Description

These sorts of questions are easy to answer. Your question might say something like:

Describe how the theme of courage is seen in the book *To Kill a Mockingbird*.

Or:

Describe how the French Revolution was helpful to the working classes.

With the pure description question, you need to describe a

particular theme, character, or event in a book or play and the effect of this theme, character, or event in that book or play. Yes, it's a straightforward type of question. But don't just describe the event or theme and give a boring retelling of the storyline. Think about what might be the MOST important of all the things that you are describing, and emphasise that in your essay.

> The ability to stand back and look at a topic and think about what is more important is a key analytical skill, and a characteristic of top essay writers. Start to develop it.

2. The Double Whammy

A double whammy question is one essay question but it has two distinct parts. What the teacher is expecting you to do is to answer each part of the question. Here's an example of one:

Discuss the reasons for migration after World War II. Why were some countries more popular than others?

Now, the sneaky thing is that this sounds like *one* question, and it is. But it has *two* distinct parts: Discuss the reasons for migration after World War II. AND THEN: Why were some countries more popular than others?

> The key thing to look for in a double whammy question is the presence of TWO sentences or phrases: EACH sentence or phrase requiring you to do something.

To answer this sort of question, you need to do both halves of the question—and unless you are told otherwise, you should assume that you spend half of your essay dealing with the first part of the question, and half of your essay dealing with the second phrase, or sentence, in the question.

The clue for when you might not do this is if you see that little word BRIEFLY. For instance, if the question had said:

- -

Briefly discuss the reasons for migration after World War II. Why were some countries more popular than others?

- -

Then you would know that you only have to lightly mention the reasons for migration, but that the real meat of the question—AND where all the marks are sitting—is in the second half, the reasons for some countries being more popular than others.

3. The Think Critical

The 'think critical' is the classic essay question—because it wants you to write an in-depth and well-argued answer. This sort of question does not want you just to retell the events, or write in a half-hearted sort of way. The think critical is wanting you to take a firm stand—make a strong claim—and then write an informative answer showing the marker why this is so.

A big clue in these styles of questions is the word ANALYSE—or EXAMINE—in the question. Sometimes, and especially as you move on in your studies, the word CRITICALLY might also be thrown in. So you might get a question that reads:

- -

Critically analyse how Shakespeare uses humour to sway the audience in the play *Much Ado About Nothing*.

- -

Your job is not only to think about the times that Shakespeare uses humour in the play and how it affects the audience. You also need to consider things like:

★ How effective are the instances when humour is employed?

★ Does humour really influence the audience and side them with one character or another?

★ Are there times when Shakespeare (or whoever the author might be) uses humour more effectively than at others?

You are being asked to THINK in the think critical question. Come to an overall position on which is the best idea and why. Or, the most effective and why. In this sort of question, all the time you are demonstrating that you are thinking carefully about this material you are writing your essay on, and not just accepting, at a superficial level, what you read.

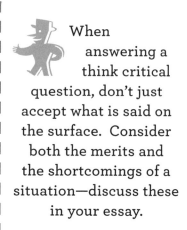

When answering a think critical question, don't just accept what is said on the surface. Consider both the merits and the shortcomings of a situation—discuss these in your essay.

4. The Quote

In this question an important quote is picked from a book or play and set as an essay topic. Let me give you some examples. Your question might read something like:

'The most important skill in life is common sense.' Discuss.
'Respect is to be earned, not given.' Discuss.
'Romance is at the heart of all great poetry.' Discuss.

All these sorts of questions are asking you to do the same thing. The teacher is picking a quote that touches on topics, ideas, or themes that you have been discussing in your classwork. But the question they are setting you is so broad they are presenting it like a challenge. Challenging you to see what you can make of it.

In essence they are saying to you: 'I know you are a bright

student. And I know you are a good thinker. I don't mind what ideas you emphasise or discuss about this quote, I just want you to pick some aspect of it and discuss it in a well-argued essay, showing me how or why this is the case.'

These are fun questions, because you have the opportunity to really take ownership of them. Just make sure you gather together good information, and are ready to answer your question thoughtfully and well.

5. The 'What Makes' Question

Sometimes you get a question that suggests a particular view, good or bad, about the topic. The question might say, for example:

- -

What makes Ronaldo such a likeable character in the play?

- -

With the 'what makes' question your teacher might pick any one of a number of words, and drop it into the question. As I show below, they might ask: What makes (George, Henrietta, etc.) such a (likeable / awful) character in the (book / poem)?

It doesn't matter what words the teacher drops into the question.

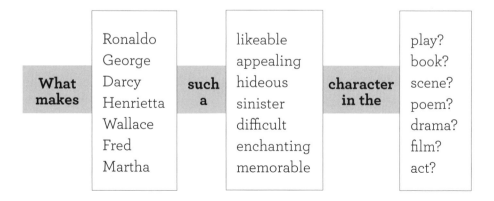

| **What makes** | Ronaldo
George
Darcy
Henrietta
Wallace
Fred
Martha | **such a** | likeable
appealing
hideous
sinister
difficult
enchanting
memorable | **character in the** | play?
book?
scene?
poem?
drama?
film?
act? |

The STYLE of question remains the same. You have two choices with such a question. You can:

1) Write an essay arguing the points for WHY Ronaldo is such a likeable character in the book / play / film, etc.
2) Or, write an essay saying why you DO NOT find Ronaldo such a likeable character—and instead find him a dislikeable character— and argue your points why this is so.

Either of these approaches will work with this style of question, because they all say that you are THINKING about the question and the book / play / poem / event.

6. The 'How Does' Question

The 'how does' question is a variation of the 'what makes' question. The important difference is that the teacher is wanting you to discuss the 'techniques' that the writer / playwright / filmmaker uses to create a particular effect—see the difference?

Have a look at the variations of the 'how does' question below. All of them are asking you to discuss the various literary techniques (or cinematic techniques, if a film question) that are used by the writer / playwright / poet to achieve the particular effect that the question is focusing on.

| How does | Shakespeare
Hemingway
Austen
Spielberg
Dickens
Tolstoy
Brontë
Longfellow | create
such a | powerful
evocative
welcoming
memorable
challenging
unforgettable
foreboding
pleasant | atmoshere
in the | play?
book?
scene?
poem?
drama?
film?
act? |

Can you see how a teacher (or examiner) can just drop a different word into the various parts of the question to ask you a different question?

So, for example, if your question was: How does Tolstoy create such a powerful atmosphere in the book *War and Peace*? Your job is NOT to write about interesting scenes in the book. Your job is to write about the WAYS that TOLSTOY creates the powerful atmosphere in the book. How does he do it? Does he use metaphor, personification, imagery, foreshadowing, speech, introspective narrative, dramatic events? Each of the techniques you discuss in your essay can be a separate paragraph. In each paragraph you need to examine how Tolstoy uses the technique and WHAT the EFFECT of the technique is in the book and on the reader.

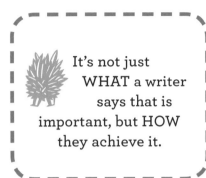

It's not just WHAT a writer says that is important, but HOW they achieve it.

7. The 'How Far' Question

The last style of question you might get asked that I discuss in this book is the 'how far' question. This is a favourite with history examiners.

In the 'how far' question, the teacher or examiner is wanting you

| How far did | Europe
Churchill
France
Germany
the UN
Nationalism
Napoleon
industrialisation | suffer
prosper
succeed
benefit
develop
fail
expand
change | in the years | prior to WWI?
after the plague?
before his death?
1961–62?
during the revolution?
in his presidency?
during the Depression?
after 1850? |

to ASSESS to what degree something was achieved or not. They DON'T want you to blindly agree with the direction of the question. Instead, they want you to think about to what extent the statement in the question was achieved.

In your essay, then, they want you to discuss the ways in which the statement expressed in the question was true AND the extent to which the statement was or was not achieved. That is, they want you to discuss BOTH sides of the question: the way it was achieved, and the way it might not have been.

Then, in the conclusion of your essay, they are looking for you to restate the question in your own words, based on the information you have presented in the essay. To say something like:

While we might say Nationalism was successful in the years prior to WWI, as this essay has shown, Nationalism's greatest success was to emerge in the years following conflict when wider democracy supported nationalistic ideals.

BE SPECIFIC

For any of the above approaches to your essay question, THINK THROUGH WHAT IS THE MOST IMPORTANT POINT you are making.

There are a number of things that we could talk about in an essay, but they are not all of equal importance in our mind. Knowing what to say in an essay is made easier if you can think about WHAT'S the MOST IMPORTANT thing I want to say. And then say it.

PLANNING
TECHNIQUES

Planning Your Work

One of the things that good writers always do is plan. I know it sounds tedious, and a bit like you might be wasting some of your precious writing time. But you aren't. Actually, you will waste more time just sitting there, trying to think of the next intelligent thing to say. If you had a plan this wouldn't happen.

Expert writers work to a plan. Their writing happens faster and makes more sense because of it. So use a technique the professionals use: take some time and plan what you are going to write.

> **Writing a plan will help you:**
> a) Write more logically.
> b) Write to a particular direction—that is, what you write will have a clear point.
> c) Write more coherently—your ideas will link together.
> d) Write faster—you will get your writing work done in less time.

Spending hours on some elaborate plan is a waste of time. The first time you try, it might take you 10-20 minutes. That's okay. As you get used to planning your essays, you will speed up considerably, to the point where you will be able to knock up a quick essay plan in three or four minutes. Let's look at how this will happen.

The List Plan

Even just something as straightforward as a list of ideas can be converted into a plan. To do this, list on a piece of paper all the ideas that you think you would like to write about in your essay. When you have finished, sit back and look at them. Here's a list plan exploring economic development in the USSR under Stalin:

Write your initial list

> ### USSR economic development under Stalin
>
> — Trotsky ousted
>
> — Few safety standards in factories
>
> — Stalin outmanoeuvres other committee members
>
> — 5-year plans for economic development
>
> — Large increases in coal, oil, and iron production
>
> — By 1921 Russian economy collapsed
>
> — Many factory workers illiterate
>
> — Famine in 1932–1934
>
> — Introduction of collectivism
>
> — Purges—people sent to slave labour camps (gulag)
>
> — 1941 USSR second strongest industrial power in the world

The list is useful, because you can see a whole inventory of interesting ideas. To convert the list into an essay plan, there are two things you need to do, as described below.

Refine your list

First, run down your list and write a number 1 next to the first thing that you would like to discuss in your essay. Then, write the number 2 beside the next thing you would like to discuss. Do this consecutively, numbering the ideas off according to how many paragraphs you have to write. If your essay is five paragraphs long, then your list should have the numbers 1, 2, 3, 4, 5 next to relevant ideas on the list.

If there are any ideas on your list that are closely associated with each other (as you can see on mine below), you can use the same number twice. Remember, each number corresponds to a paragraph in your essay, so if you see information that you might

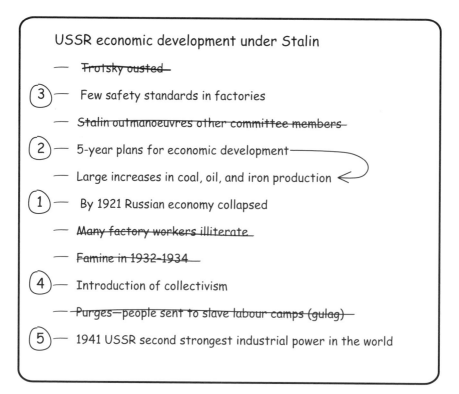

like to include in paragraph 2, for example, add an arrow to that information.

Second, cross off all the information on your list that you do not wish to incorporate in your essay.

Your list plan is now complete. You have considered WHAT you want to include in your essay, the BEST order of the information, and what ideas to LEAVE OUT. When you come to write, you know what to write about, and the best order in which to write about it.

The Box Plan

This is one of my favourites. I call it the 'box plan' because every paragraph is a box in the plan. To make such a plan, simply draw the number of boxes on a page equal to the number of paragraphs that you have to write. If your essay is to be 600 words long, draw 6 boxes.

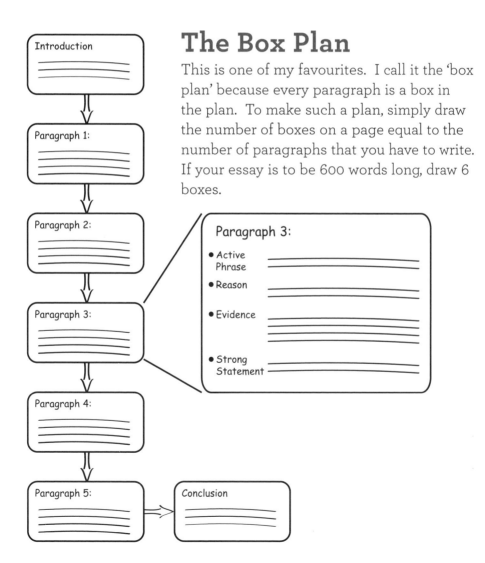

The first box is your introduction, so write the word introduction in that box. The final box is your conclusion, so write the word conclusion inside that box.

Then, in the top of the remaining boxes, you write the main idea that you would like to write about in that paragraph. Underneath this main idea, jot down two or three facts or pieces of information about this idea which will help you write the paragraph.

In this manner, you have constructed an essay plan that includes the topics you will discuss as well as lists the relevant pieces of evidence you will include in your essay—so you are ready to start writing.

The Advanced Box Plan

For a more advanced version of the box plan, try rephrasing the main point of each of your paragraphs as an active phrase.

For example, say that one of your paragraphs was going to discuss 'Stalin's 5-year plans' and this was the main topic of your paragraph. If you were to rephrase this as an active phrase you might write something like:

- -

How Stalin's 5-year plans enabled socialism to become established.

- -

Or here's another version:

- -

Why Stalin's 5-year plans were crucial to establishing socialism.

- -

It is an active phrase because you are saying WHAT you intend to SHOW about the main topic. Writing a main point like this can make it easier to keep your paragraph focused.

If you want to rewrite a main point for a paragraph as an active phrase, try starting the active phrase with the word 'How' or the word 'Why'. It is much easier.

HINT

Before you say your box plan is complete,
look at all your filled-in boxes, and think
for a moment: Do the boxes flow in the
best order? If, when you look at it, you
think that the ideas in box 4 would really work far better
nearer the start of the essay, and the ideas in box 2 would
make more sense nearer the end, simply renumber the boxes.

Tools to Help You Plan

For any book, play, or film that you study, try writing yourself an 'ideas sheet'. It will help you in two ways: firstly, it will help you think about the key ideas in the literary work; secondly, an ideas sheet is a great resource when it comes to writing essays, or studying for exams.

An Ideas Sheet

Author   (write the name, and make sure you spell it correctly!)

Title   (of the book or play or film)

Brief Summary   (write a brief outline of what the book or play or film is about: This book describes . . .)

Setting   (where the book or play or film takes place)

Plot   (what happens in the story, for example: A revolution takes place, during which the hero realises that his father is not his real father, but in fact his true father is the leader of the invading forces. The hero defends his people, loses a duel with his true father, and then, in a climactic battle, rids the country of the invading forces (while finding true love). (Sounds a lot like a galaxy far, far, away doesn't it . . .?))

Characters   (list the main characters—noting 8 words to describe each of the characters)

Key Themes   (jot down the key themes for the work: love, romance, marriage, revenge, social injustice, etc.)

Quotes   (one per theme: find one short quote that illustrates each of the key themes in the book)

This whole fact sheet should be no longer than two sides of an A4 piece of paper. Or, if you can do it on one side of an A3 piece and stick it on your wall, even better.

Doing a Character Profile

If you are studying a book or a play, one of the things you need to grasp is how the characters work in with the theme of the book, or how the theme of the book is shown through different characters.

Drawing a quick 'character profile' will help you do this and it only takes a few minutes.

How to Do It

a)   Grab a large sheet of paper. On it, write down the names of all the main characters in the book or play or film at the top of the page.

b). Pen a short paragraph describing the role of each character in the book or play or film.

c)   Under this, write a list of words that describe each character. Think hard. Don't just write words like bad, kind, good. Be thoughtful. Are they malicious, doubting, scheming, loyal, dependable, unscrupulous?

d)   Then, below that, list the key themes of the book that this character connects to. That is, what the author or playwright

Character Profile

Character 1	Character 2	Character 3
Key qualities: _____ _____ _____	Key qualities: _____ _____ _____	Key qualities: _____ _____ _____
Role: _____ _____ _____	Role: _____ _____ _____	Role: _____ _____ _____
Themes: _____ _____ _____	Themes: _____ _____ _____	Themes: _____ _____ _____
Short quotes: _____ _____ _____	Short quotes: _____ _____ _____	Short quotes: _____ _____ _____

highlights through this character.

e) Finally, beneath all that, jot down three short quotes for each character that illustrate some of those themes.

Here's an example:

Character Profile: David Killywood

Key qualities:

* ★   fretful
* ★   unimaginative
* ★   generous
* ★   loyal
* ★   tense
* ★   fearless

Role in book:

David is the contrast or foil to the main character, Henry Boyce. David's consistent kindness in the book makes us realise that courage is worth it, and that loyalty can help bind a family together— even one that is torn apart by terrible class conflict.

Connects to themes of:
- ★ courage
- ★ family
- ★ class conflict

Key quotes:
'I will never stop until we are all equal!'
'Why didn't I think of that?'
'I am sorry that happened to you. I don't think I meant it.'

CHARACTER PROFILES ARE GREAT EXAM PREP

A quick character profile will help you remember a number of important things as you prepare for your exam:

a) You will use better words to describe characters—better language helps to earn higher grades. Use a thesaurus.

b) You will be able to show HOW the characters connect to the themes of the work. That is, if you are discussing a theme in the book, you will have ready examples to draw on because you will have thought about how different characters are related to those themes.

c) You will learn some relevant quotes that will help you in your exam answer.

The 3 Big Ideas Essay Plan

Here's something that I have found helpful over the years: I call it my '3 Big Ideas' essay plan. Often you are given an essay topic, and you end up sitting there wondering what on earth you are going to write about: either you have too many possible ideas (and you are stuck wondering which ones to put in the essay and which ones to leave out); or you might be sitting there thinking: 'I don't know the first thing to say in this essay—I'll never complete it!'

Let me give you this useful little tip to get you over the essay hump. When you get your essay question, sit down and think of 3 THINGS you can say about this question. Just 3 ideas. No more. Each of these points becomes a paragraph in your essay. Find some evidence to back up each of your 3 points and away you go.

Go for depth in your essay writing rather than breadth: you will score more highly as a result.

Introduction

Big idea 1: _____

Big idea 2: _____

Big idea 3: _____

Conclusion

If you have to write a longer essay, don't think up more points to argue. Instead, think of alternative ways to support the 3 KEY POINTS you are making. Present your ideas from a different perspective. Discuss the same idea using a different event, or an alternative character.

In short, you are going to write deeper rather than broader. But all the time, you write your essay concentrating on conveying 3 IDEAS well, rather than, say, 15 different ideas in less depth.

Why do you do this? Because essays that go for depth always score more highly than essays that write broadly (and more shallowly) about a topic. Have a go.

WRITING AN
INTRODUCTION

The 4-Sentence Introduction

So far in this book we have discussed what an essay really is, examined how to overcome starting problems, and covered some planning techniques. Now it's time to start your introduction, and in this section I'm going to show you how to do this **sentence by sentence**.

Introductions

An essay introduction has two functions:

1) It has to introduce the topic.
2) It has to tell the person reading the essay what the essay is about.

To accomplish both of these objectives you do not need to write a long introduction. In fact, you can write a first-rate introduction in just 4 sentences and achieve these twin aims.

An Introduction in 4 Sentences
Sentence 1: neutral sentence

The first sentence you can write in your essay introduction is a neutral sentence. In English, a neutral sentence is a sentence of which the facts are generally agreed. It is a sentence that is not open to dispute. The nice thing about a neutral sentence is that it is simple to write, and an easy way to begin your essay. Here are some examples of neutral sentences:

★ Many nineteenth-century poets had romantic imagery at the core of their poems.
★ Shakespeare was one of England's greatest playwrights.
★ The American Civil War ruptured the country into two clear sides.
★ Social conflict is a central theme in many modern novels.
★ Expanding foreign trade is an important element in any country's economic growth.

The above sentences are all neutral sentences. They just make a general statement that everyone can agree on. The key is that, in less than a minute, you have written the first sentence of your essay.

For the purposes of example, let's say that I was writing an essay on England's Industrial Revolution. My question is: Discuss the economic and social gains of the English Industrial Revolution. Here's a neutral sentence I could start my essay with:

- -

The English Industrial Revolution (1750–1850) transformed the economic and cultural fabric of English society.

- -

The aim of the sentence is not to convince the reader of anything, merely to commence the essay in an informative way.

Sentence 2: context sentence

In the second sentence of the introduction you place your essay topic in a broader context. Show the person reading your essay that you understand this topic and know something about it. For the English Industrial Revolution example, you might write something like:

- -

Innovation in textile production and advances in iron and steel production saw manufacturing rapidly overtake agricultural output.

- -

Sentence 3: state the argument sentence

The third sentence of your introduction states the argument of your essay. Being absolutely clear, tell the person reading what viewpoint you are adopting in the essay. Here's the Industrial Revolution example:

> This essay will argue that despite important gains in industrialisation serious social problems such as overcrowding and pollution lowered English living standards.

From this sentence you now know exactly what I am going to talk about in my essay, and the side of the argument I am taking.

For sentence 3 of your introduction, you can use phrases like 'This essay will argue . . .' or 'This essay will show . . .'. They are common practice among good writers, and they help you think about precisely what it is that you intend to say.

When you have finished your introduction, read it out loud then ask yourself this question: Is it clear what my essay is going to be about? You should be able to say: YES.

Sentence 4: summing up sentence

The last sentence of your introduction sums up your essay. It is your chance to drive home the point that you intend to argue in your essay. You can make a strong statement, or, if you like, use words like 'Overall, . . .' or 'In sum, . . .' to introduce your final sentence. This tells the reader that you are concluding the introductory paragraph. In the Industrial Revolution example, my last sentence reads:

> Overall, gains in wealth came at the expense of the health and welfare of the lower classes.

This last sentence drives home my position in the argument. I am saying: Yes, the Industrial Revolution offered some gains, but these came at a cost to the lower classes of society that was unacceptable.

Putting it all together

Here's my introduction all pieced together.

Essay question:

Discuss the economic and social gains of the English Industrial Revolution.

My introduction:

> The English Industrial Revolution (1750–1850) transformed the economic and cultural fabric of English society. Innovation in textile production and advances in iron and steel production saw manufacturing rapidly overtake agricultural output. This essay will argue that despite important gains in industrialisation serious social problems such as overcrowding and pollution lowered English living standards. Overall, gains in wealth came at the expense of the health and welfare of the lower classes.

Try reciting your introduction to a friend and see if they can tell you precisely what your essay is going to be about, and the main point you are making. If they can, you have written a top-class introduction.

Present Your Best Introduction

Don't Describe the Process: State Your Argument

There's one more thing you MUST learn about writing introductions. When you write an introduction, don't fall into the trap of telling your reader HOW you intend to tackle the question (the process), tell them your argument!

For example, say you were studying Jane Austen's *Pride and Prejudice* and you were given the following question:

How does Austen show her views on marriage in the book *Pride and Prejudice*?

Some people will write an introduction like this:

Jane Austen was a compelling nineteenth-century novelist whose portrayal of English country life often featured courtship and marriage. This essay will discuss how Austen reveals her views on marriage in the book *Pride and Prejudice*.

That sort of writing is a C-grade response. Forget the interesting first sentence. Immediately, without reading any further in the essay, an experienced marker will know that the person did not know how to write a top-class essay because of the second sentence. This second sentence gives you no idea what the essay will be about—it merely tells you the essay process.

Now have a look at the following version. Some people write this sort of introduction:

Jane Austen was a compelling nineteenth-century novelist whose portrayal of English country life often featured courtship and marriage. This essay will discuss how Austen reveals her views on marriage in the book *Pride and Prejudice* by looking at different characters and events in the book.

This is a B-level response. Yes, it is a step further on than the previous version, but it still only tells me the **process** you intend to follow in your essay. I learn nothing of how you **really feel** about the question, or what the **main points** of your essay are. Of course, in your head you know already what you want to say, but you are not telling anyone. You are just telling us how you intend to go about it, not what you intend to say. And you need to tell us. Make it clear and upfront.

Now check out this version:

Jane Austen was a compelling nineteenth-century novelist whose portrayal of English country life often featured courtship and marriage. This essay will argue that Austen explored three types of marriage in the book *Pride and Prejudice* to demonstrate that the best sort of marriage, Elizabeth and Darcy's, was one based on true affection and mutual respect.

Same question—but this time an A-grade introduction. It is crystal clear what the essay is going to be about. You see, it doesn't matter **what** you intend to argue in your essay, what matters is that you make it absolutely **clear** to the reader in the **first paragraph** what your argument is. Here are two further examples:

- -

Jane Austen was a compelling nineteenth-century novelist whose portrayal of English country life often featured courtship and marriage. This essay will argue that Austen uses satire and humour to show that a truly happy marriage is only possible when reason and thoughtfulness are balanced with affection and passion.

- -

In the next version I drop the phrase 'This essay will argue . . .', as some teachers prefer this. But the approach to the introduction remains the same. Both are A-grade introductions because they tell the reader WHAT the essay is going to argue.

- -

Jane Austen was a compelling nineteenth-century novelist whose portrayal of English country life often featured courtship and marriage. In *Pride and Prejudice* Austen rejects the social patterns of the time and shows that marriage should be based on true affection and respect instead of wealth or class.

- -

Even though you have never read either of the above essays, just from the introduction you can tell precisely what each essay will discuss.

THE BODY
PARAGRAPH

The Body Paragraph: Using Evidence

Once you have written the introduction of your essay, it is now time to write the body paragraphs. In the following pages, I am going to show you how to do this. But before we get there, we need to consider evidence.

A great essay uses evidence to build its case and show why the points that it is arguing are sound. There are basically three types of evidence you can use in your essay:

1) Facts and figures
2) Case examples
3) Expert opinion (quotes)

Let's look at each in detail.

Facts and Figures

Facts: names, dates, places, amounts, etc. Facts give your essay depth and authenticity.

Don't write:

- -

Napoleon finally got back from Moscow with only a few of his army left.

- -

Instead, write the sentence like this:

- -

Napoleon's harrowing retreat from Moscow in 1812 ended with only 20,000 survivors remaining from the 450,000 troops he took into Russia six months earlier.

- -

The first example merely makes a general statement that, while true, will earn you no marks in an essay. The second example is crisp with a few well-placed facts: a top-class sentence.

Case Examples

Case examples are mini examples of the point that you are trying to make in your paragraph. They might be a particular event in a book that you want to describe in finer detail to illustrate a particular point; or an analysis of a character, or of a scene, or some lines in a poem—anything that you use as a specific example of a general point you are making in your paragraph. Here's an example:

- -

Boedley was a difficult character in the book, especially during his journey into the mid-west. For example, his constant bickering with his sister over their nine-week trek put him offside with the entire party. Added to this, Boedley's crass joking and obstinate refusal even to do the most basic of camp chores meant that the other characters felt a sense of vindication when he tumbled into the Mississippi River and was washed two miles downstream. For the long-suffering party, this event signalled that there was indeed a spirit of justice in the new world they were entering.

- -

Quotes

This can be quotes from a book or play or poem that you are studying. Or quotes can be expert opinions: the views of scholars who have written on the topic you are studying that you then discuss in your paragraph. The key when using quotes is that you don't just present the quote then move on to the next topic in your essay. You must discuss what it means and why it is relevant to your question.

> In a case example, you take a particular scene, character, or event and write about it in more detail, all the time relating it back to the point you are trying to make.

So don't just write:

Emerson says: 'Every great achievement is the victory of a flaming heart.'

If I am the person reading your essay, I will think: 'That's a nice quote—but does she really know what Emerson means by this statement?'

Instead, write something like this:

Emerson says: 'Every great achievement is the victory of a flaming heart.' What Emerson meant by this was that passion must be at the heart of what we do if we are to achieve great accomplishments. It is no good doing something simply out of obligation or compulsion. To truly attain significance, our work must flow from a heart-felt passion.

Now you are starting to write! And scoring marks.

Vary Your Evidence

When you write your essay, you can also vary the evidence that you use. If you were writing an English literature essay, for example, in one paragraph you might use a mini case example of a particular scene in a book. In another paragraph, you could discuss how the author portrays one of the key characters. Then, in a further paragraph, pull together facts and figures to show how the author created pace and drama in the novel. And finally, using a quote from a scene, analyse the literary techniques used in those words, discussing them in your essay.

If you are writing a poetry essay, evidence still matters. Your teacher wants to see how your emotions were affected by the poem, so you will be more personal in your writing in a poetry essay than most other essays. But your thoughts and views will still connect to an analysis of the words, the form, the imagery, the structure, the literary techniques applied to the poem by the poet. In other words, you are still using evidence to support your views.

PREC: A Helpful Body Paragraph Approach

Here is one technique for writing a body paragraph: I call it PREC.

> **P** Point
>
> **R** Reason
>
> **E** Example
>
> **C** Concluding Sentence

★ **Point**: in your first sentence state the point that you are making in your paragraph.

★ **Reason**: in your second sentence state the reason WHY that point is significant (important to the question).

★ **Example**: now spend two sentences giving an example to illustrate your point.

★ **Concluding Sentence**: finish with a concluding sentence, then move on to the next POINT, in the next paragraph.

Here is a paragraph written to this style. Look for what the different sentences are achieving (I have put their function in square brackets at the end of each sentence).

Author Jack Patton drew on his varied life experiences for his novels. [That was my POINT sentence]. This was significant because his many occupations allowed him to discuss in realistic detail different topics during his 30-year writing career. [That was my REASON sentence—why the point was important—here comes my EXAMPLE]. For example, Patton's novel about an Egyptian business family, *Cairo Voyage*, was helped by his experiences as a travel writer in the 1960s. Equally, in Patton's book *Airplane* the main character, William Murphy, draws on Patton's own background as a WWII fighter pilot, where he learned the routines of aerial combat. [Here comes my CONCLUDING COMMENT]. From gripping life experiences like these, Patton's believable characters and authentic plots pull the reader into the fabric of his novels.

> A mini case study does not have to be long in a paragraph to make a point convincingly and earn you good marks.

Here's another example: A history paragraph about the impact of technological developments in the Second Industrial Revolution—and this time I am going to drop in a mini case study about Sir Henry Bessemer.

Improvements in production processes sped on the Second Industrial Revolution. [POINT]. Significantly, innovation in the steel industry allowed cheaper and easier production of steel, and brought some inventors great wealth. [That was the REASON it was important—now I am going to give my EXAMPLE]. For example, English engineer Sir Henry Bessemer discovered that by blowing oxygen through melted cast iron the iron heated and purified. His process, announced in 1856, allowed for the production of high-grade, relatively inexpensive steel. Bessemer received more than £1m for his invention. [Here comes my CONCLUDING COMMENT—which I want to use as a link to my next paragraph]. But it was not just about the money—Bessemer's crucial invention enabled the construction of safer and more durable steel structures.

- -

Try this formula in your own work as you write body paragraphs. As you become more confident, of course, you can vary your approach. But remember: discuss only **one idea per paragraph**, and be **specific with your evidence** to support the idea that you are discussing.

A Little More Advice on Using Quotes

Quotes are great in an essay. They work, and add interest to your writing, but there are some IMPORTANT rules about using quotes that you MUST follow if you want to score TOP GRADES.

Rules for Quotes

Use short quotes

Don't use long quotes. A quote of 4 or 5 words, discussed well, is much better than a quote of 3 lines. You don't get essay marks for **remembering** quotes—you get them for **explaining** the quote.

Tell what the quote means

You MUST always tell the reader of your essay what the quote means. DO this immediately following the quote. You may be overt about this and say: 'Meaning . . .' or, 'This quote suggests . . .' or, 'What this quote means is . . .', but if you don't tell the reader what the quote means, they will assume that you don't know either.

ALWAYS analyse your quote

Analysing your quote means that you tell the marker in a sentence or two, no more, how the quote applies to the question at hand—how it relates to the point you are making; why it is relevant.

Do the above three things and you will always use quotes correctly. And yes, if you hadn't figured it out already, a nice short quote, by the time you tell me what it means and then how it relates to the question, writing a couple of good, thoughtful sentences, actually makes a paragraph. So there you go. Find a good quote and write a whole useful 5-sentence paragraph (including the quote).

Here are two examples so you know what I mean:

- -

Though the Allies successfully invaded the beaches of Normandy in 1944, success was by no means assured. The invasion had not gone to plan, and American forces at Omaha Beach suffered heavily. Churchill's dictum seemed apt: 'War is mainly a catalogue of blunders.' What Churchill meant by this was that the best planning and strategies only help so far, and in the confusion and desperation of war, there are often lots of mistakes. This was certainly the case at Omaha Beach. Fortunately, the early gains in the first week of Normandy suggested that there were more successes than blunders in this regard.

- -

The second body paragraph uses a quote from Harper Lee's *To Kill a Mockingbird*:

- -

Courage is a dominant theme in *Mockingbird*, and one that Harper Lee brings out forcefully in the character of Atticus. Atticus's courage, both in action and in word, serves to keep a spirit of optimism in the book, and draws the reader deeper in the hope that good will overcome. 'You rarely win,' said Atticus, 'but sometimes you do,' suggests that even though Atticus believed that the situation looked bad for Tom Robinson, it was still possible to have a just outcome. And as the character of Boo Radley emerges from his shell, we are led to believe such a victory is possible even more.

- -

WRITING
CONCLUSIONS

Conclusions

Some people find it challenging to write a conclusion. They think: 'I've said everything that I want to say in the essay—what on earth am I going to say in the conclusion?'

Conclusions are your opportunity to look back across your whole essay, and also drive home the points that you are trying to make. Importantly, they are the place where you can bring in strong, thoughtful comments—because your hard work in the essay gives you the right to do so.

If you struggle with the idea of writing a conclusion, here is a 4-sentence approach that will work for your essay writing in high school.

Sentence 1: Restate Your Argument

Restate what your essay has argued. To write this sort of sentence, firstly, go back to the introduction that you penned at the start. Have a look at sentence 3 in your introductory paragraph. There, you wrote what the argument of your essay was. This sentence can be the basis for sentence 1 of your conclusion, which you can merely rewrite in a slightly more interesting way.

You might say something like:

This essay has argued that while Europe did struggle from the effects of WWI, these difficulties were not widely felt.

Or:

This essay has shown how Austen's views on marriage were most powerfully revealed through Elizabeth and Darcy's courtship.

Or, you could simply say, if you wanted to:

Austen's views on marriage were most powerfully shown through Elizabeth and Darcy's courtship.

Sentence 2: Tell How You Demonstrated Your Argument

In sentence 2 of your conclusion tell the reader how you showed your main argument in your essay. What did you discuss?

You might write something like:

In particular, the essay has shown that while the French and Belgian economies struggled after four years of conflict, areas such as Spain, the Netherlands, and Scandinavia were relatively unscathed.

Or:

In particular, the essay has shown that the poverty of relationship experienced by the Bennets and Mr and Mrs Collins served to accentuate the quality of marriage enjoyed by Elizabeth and Darcy.

Your conclusion is your opportunity to be bold, strong, thoughtful, and provocative about the ideas that you have presented in your essay.

See how I homed in on one point in particular to make my comment?

Sentence 3: Thoughtful Analysis

In sentence 3, bring out the main point in your whole essay. You can state, of all the things you discussed in your essay, which was the most important and why.

This is the part of the conclusion where you can also make a strong personal statement. Offer some thoughtful analysis, or a personal response to the question being asked.

For the history question, you might write:

- -

Trade was a vital factor, and the fact that industry and production in non-combatant nations rose to 150 per cent of their pre-1914 levels enabled a rapid economic recovery in these areas.

- -

Or, a more personal response for the English literature example:

- -

Though they clearly encountered difficulties overcoming their ingrained prejudices, I was drawn to the sincerity and honesty that Darcy and Elizabeth finally enjoyed.

- -

Sentence 4: Strong Statement

Finish with a strong comment to end your essay on a bold note. You have presented a logical, thoughtful piece of writing that is well written and full of good evidence. Having done all this hard work, you have earned the right to make a strong statement about your topic at the end of your essay. Sometimes, it is appropriate to restate the question that was originally asked, putting your particular slant on the question given the work that you have done in the essay already. Have a look at the following as examples of some of those strong statement sentences to conclude your great essay.

For the history question:

Conflict, while fulfilling nationalist desires to enlarge territories and influence, ultimately proved disastrous for the economic stability of Europe.

Or, for the English literature version:

Marriage, though constrained by Victorian beliefs, could be far more fulfilling than just a social custom or route to wealth.

In total, the two conclusions we've been working on through this section would read:

This essay has argued that while Europe did struggle from the effects of WWI, these difficulties were not widely felt. In particular, the essay has shown that while the French and Belgian economies struggled after four years of conflict, areas such as Spain, the Netherlands, and Scandinavia were relatively unscathed. Trade was a vital factor, and the fact that industry and production in non-combatant nations rose to 150 per cent of their pre-1914 levels enabled a rapid economic recovery in these areas. Conflict, while fulfilling nationalist desires to enlarge territories and influence, ultimately proved disastrous for the economic stability of Europe.

Or:

This essay has shown how Austen's views on marriage were most powerfully revealed through Elizabeth and Darcy's courtship. In particular, the essay has shown that the poverty of relationship experienced by the Bennets and Mr and Mrs Collins served to accentuate the quality of marriage enjoyed by Elizabeth and Darcy. Though they clearly encountered difficulties overcoming their ingrained prejudices, I was drawn to the sincerity and honesty that Darcy and Elizabeth finally enjoyed. Marriage, though constrained by Victorian beliefs, could be far more fulfilling than just a social custom or route to wealth.

- -

And if you wanted to write the second paragraph without using phrases like 'this essay' and 'the essay', here's how you can do it:

- -

Austen's views on marriage were most powerfully revealed through Elizabeth and Darcy's courtship. In particular, the poverty of relationship experienced by the Bennets and Mr and Mrs Collins served to accentuate the quality of marriage enjoyed by Elizabeth and Darcy. Though they clearly encountered difficulties overcoming their ingrained prejudices, I was drawn to the sincerity and honesty that Darcy and Elizabeth finally enjoyed. Marriage, though constrained by Victorian beliefs, could be far more fulfilling than just a social custom or route to wealth.

- -

Be **creative** in your conclusions: talk about what you found convincing, what was compelling, what showed little merit, what surprised you, what intrigued you— it is your opportunity to write thoughtfully, considering your whole topic.

WRITING
BETTER
SENTENCES

Fundamentals of Sentence Design

As a lad, I was train mad. I would spend hours attaching engines to passenger cars or small wooden boxcars and whizzing them round my train set. Why am I telling you this? Because the sentence is like a train. The subject is the engine, and all the bits that follow the subject are like assorting carriages in different combinations after the engine.

The Sentence is Like a Train

Let me show you how it works. Let's say that the subject of your sentence is a bird. And you want to say something about that bird in your sentence. All the bits that you say about your bird are like the carriages of your train. In technical lingo, all the other bits and pieces in the sentence that come after the subject are called the 'predicate'.

The bird	sat in a tree.
Engine	**Carriage**
(Subject)	(Predicate)

The phrase 'sat in a tree' is my first carriage. Now I have an engine ('The bird') and a carriage ('sat in a tree'). I can then add to this to make the sentence longer and more interesting.

Let's add another phrase, 'watching a delicious worm'. My train now has an engine and two carriages.

The bird   sat in a tree   watching a delicious worm.
Engine   **Carriage**   **Carriage**

Okay, now here is where the fun starts, because you can alter the order of your engine and your carriages to make your sentence even more interesting. For instance, you could move your phrases around so that your engine is in the middle of the sentence:

Watching a delicious worm, the bird sat in a tree.

Note: *If you stick a carriage in front of your engine, you need to add a comma. It's the rule in English. Officially, it is called beginning your sentence with a dependent clause. Much easier to remember is: stick a carriage in front, add a comma.*

Using Adverbs

What if you want to add an adverb in front of your engine? Adverbs are (mostly) the -ly words in English. Again, the rule is if you stick something in front of your engine, you need to add a comma.

> Don't be tripped up by complex terminology about English; good sentences follow some common-sense rules.

Here are some adverbs: thoughtfully, sleepily, carefully, happily, quickly, easily, eagerly, sneakily.

So we grab an adverb (I pick 'thoughtfully') and add it in front of my engine:

> Thoughtfully, the bird sat in a tree watching a delicious worm.

Alright, now we're getting somewhere. But you aren't finished yet. You can also say things about your engine and your carriages in your sentence. Let's try the engine first. This time we are going to take a description and add it directly after the engine to say some more about the subject of the sentence.

I might write 'looking forlorn and weary', or, I could write 'with one leg and seven nostrils'. But no, I am going to play it safe, and add in my 'who had not eaten for three days'. So my sentence appears:

> Thoughtfully, the bird, who had not eaten for three days, sat in a tree watching a delicious worm.

Did you see how I added some more commas? If you take a description of the subject and place it after your engine, you need to **insert a comma either side of your carriage**. This is another example of what English professors call a dependent clause. This basically means that you have a group of words which describe something in your sentence but are dependent for their meaning on the phrase or clause or word that came before. Because of this, you can insert or remove dependent clauses in a sentence with no harm to the overall sentence whatsoever.

> Learn the basic rule behind how to drop 'carriages' in and out of sentences. Your writing will begin to take on a whole new vigour.

The test rule is that you can place your finger over the dependent clause and the sentence still reads okay. Have a look at the following. For each of them, I have just placed a different carriage after my engine.

- -

★ Thoughtfully, the bird, who had not eaten for three days, sat in a tree watching a delicious worm.

★ Thoughtfully, the bird, munching on a sandwich while he read his favourite book, sat in a tree watching a delicious worm.

★ Thoughtfully, the bird, recently arrived from Australia on holiday with his four cousins, sat in a tree watching a delicious worm.

- -

Elaborating the End of a Sentence

Now let's add some more details about our worm at the end of the sentence. What about if we want to describe him some more and tell people what an appetising-looking fellow he is?

My carriage is going to say 'crawl slowly along the grass'. So now we get:

- -

Thoughtfully, the bird, recently arrived from Australia on holiday with his four cousins, sat in a tree watching a delicious worm crawl slowly along the grass.

- -

Now this is getting really interesting. In fact, I get so excited about it all, I stick two more carriages on the end of my sentence while no one is watching!

- -

Thoughtfully, the bird, recently arrived from Australia on holiday with his four cousins, sat in a tree watching a delicious worm with a bright red target painted on his back crawl slowly along the grass at the foot of the tree.

- -

Now I really go bananas:

Thoughtfully, the yellow and purple cluck-cluck bird, recently arrived from Australia on holiday with his four cousins, sat in a leafy oak tree watching a delicious chocolate-brown worm with a bright red target painted on his back crawl slowly along the grass at the foot of the tree, unaware of his impending danger, and oblivious to the fact that he was about to be eaten for lunch, whether he liked it or not, by the greediest birds in the forest that morning, who really should have been doing their schoolwork and not playing with the worms.

Now you know the rules of sentence construction, don't do what I did just then and go silly on the number of carriages you add to your sentence. Good sentences are also about length. If you want to write well, keep your sentences, on average, to 20 words or less. You will produce better writing. It will be easier for people to read. And it will be more powerful.

If you want to say something else, don't bolt too many carriages onto your engine. Start another sentence and build a second train. Get it?

10 Types of Sentences You Can Write

Good writers vary the types of sentences that they write in a paragraph. It makes your writing more interesting. And, as you learn to use them, you will discover that you can say things more powerfully and with greater impact.

So here's a list of ten different sorts of sentences.

1. The Simple Sentence

Simple sentences are not sentences which are made up of easy or simple words. Simple sentences are a particular style of sentence, where the subject of the sentence is always at the start. Here are some examples:

★ The writer sat on his couch typing his first novel.
★ John ate an apple.
★ The cat lived up a tree.
★ New York is one of the world's biggest cities.
★ It is very cold this time of year.
★ They all sang the national anthem together in harmony.

Simple sentences are okay to an extent. The trouble is that when you write and string together simple sentence after simple sentence in your paragraph it becomes boring and monotonous. If you want to overcome this and begin writing with more interest and flair—and score higher grades in your work—start to vary the style of sentence that you write. So read on.

2. The Very Short Sentence

Five words or less: great for some immediate impact—but don't overuse this type of sentence or it loses its power.

★   The nation held its breath.
★   All seemed lost.
★   Hemingway paused before speaking.

3. The W-Start Sentence

Remember the 5-w's: who, what, where, why, when. Try starting a sentence with one of them—they work, and they make for interesting reading.

★   When he recovered, Atticus launched immediately into his defence.
★   Why Marconi acted like this, was yet to be discovered.
★   What was fundamental to the success of the English defenders was their sheer resilience.

4. The 2-Word Sentence

In English, there is no shorter sentence than this. It is a sentence, because it has both the subject and what the subject did.

★   Jesus wept.
★   Henry screamed.
★   Holly yawned.

5. Adverb at the Front

This sentence is made by simply sticking an adverb at the front of your sentence. It adds some interest and enjoyment to your sentence. But don't overdo this one. Too many adverbs slow writing down and make for boring reading. Use an adverb at the front of the sentence at the rate of about one per paragraph. Here are some:

★ Fortunately, Henry had eaten his dinner before the plate tumbled to the floor.
★ Easily, Donna got full marks in the test.
★ Sneakily, the wop-wop bird crept up behind the elephant hoping to devour it for dinner. (I forgot to tell you, wop-wop birds aren't very bright . . .)

6. Explore the Subject Sentence

This sentence, which you will like, is always made by starting the sentence with the subject, and then adding a description of the subject, before carrying on with the rest of the sentence.

★ Mr Brown, who usually ate all his vegetables, refused to touch his potatoes.
★ Napoleon, not renowned for his height, could not reach the top shelf in the lolly shop.
★ Willy Wonka, the loveable chocolate factory owner in Roald Dahl's book *Charlie and the Chocolate Factory*, hatched a plan to prove who was the very best child.

7. The Paired-Double

One of my favourites—and you can use it when you have a sentence containing two independent clauses and joined by a conjunction: such as *and* or *but*. An independent clause is a part of a sentence that is in fact a mini sentence which makes complete sense by itself.

If you wish to create a more forceful sentence, you can replace the 'and' with a semi-colon. Have a look:

*   *He walked into the room and there was no sign of anyone.*
*   He walked into the room; there was no sign of anyone.
*   *Caesar was angry and he still wanted to fight.*
*   Caesar was angry; he still wanted to fight.
*   *From the rich came nonsense but from the poor great wisdom.*
*   From the rich came nonsense; from the poor great wisdom.

8. Prepositional Introduction

These sorts of sentences are easy. All of them begin with a prepositional phrase at the start of the sentence. Remember: prepositions are little words indicating movement or position.

*   In the start of the book, Shaw shows clearly that social justice is a vital theme.
*   Over the river, Fred saw that salvation was at hand.
*   Behind the poetic language, Shakespeare revealed his deep anxiety.
*   Through the difficult situation, Henry developed great strength of character.

9. Verb Beginnings

Try starting a sentence with a verb. The -ing ending verbs are the easiest to do this with:

*   Running to the nearest shop, he called for assistance.
*   Devouring as much as he could, Henry could no longer contain his burp.
*   Leaving town, before anyone saw him, was the best thing Frederick could do.

10. Good ol' Red, White, and Blue

This is the sort of sentence to use when you have 2 or 3 ideas to convey about a topic. But remember the simple rule: there should be a comma before the 'and'. Have a look at these:

★ The Industrial Revolution was about innovation, ingenuity, and vision.
★ He ate strawberries, porridge, and cream all at once.
★ It was so sad that she had neither humour, nor grace, nor etiquette.
★ After it is all over, can you please pass me the red, white, and blue ice-cream so I can eat to my heart's content?

Now, go ahead and have some fun varying your sentences. Make that writing of yours more interesting, and watch those grades rise.

3 Useful Rules of Sentence Writing

(Place this on your wall)

Useful Rule Number 1: Write a Sentence—Not Half a Sentence

Write a sentence when you write a sentence—not just a bit of a sentence followed by a full stop. The good news about this rule is that it is not hard to learn what is **not a sentence**. Here comes one. Squirming for sheer life. Here's another. Going up and up and up. Here's another. Sleeping on the job. Here's one more. Finally, weather was fine.

Even just reading those sentences, you will have a hunch deep down inside that something is not right with them. And it isn't. They are incomplete. What I mean is that they are bits of a sentence, and need some other bits thrown on

These 3 simple rules will help you avoid over 50 per cent of all sentence disasters.

to complete them as sentences.

Have a look at the rewrite and you will see what I mean. First, the sentence: Going up and up and up. This is not a sentence because it has **no subject**. WHO or WHAT is going up and up and up? We don't know. If I want to make this a sentence, then I need a subject: The hot-air balloon was going up and up and up. Now, I have my sentence.

Second, the sentence: Squirming for sheer life. This is not a sentence because you have the **predicate**—what is happening to the subject—but you don't know anything about the **subject** yet—and you need one to make a sentence. So, let's add one in: The worm was squirming for sheer life as the sparrow yanked him out of the soil. Or, another version for the poor worm: The worm was squirming for sheer life as Sally dangled it from her fingers threatening to stick it down her little brother's shirt.

You see, it needed more to make it a sentence. I could have written one as short as: The worm was squirming for sheer life. That is a sentence. It isn't very interesting yet. But it passes the basic sentence tests. The sentence has a subject—the worm—and a predicate—saying something about the subject and using a verb ('was squirming for sheer life'). My verb was 'was'.

Useful Rule Number 2: Avoid Long Sentences

One of the traps that some of us fall into is that somehow, probably by thinking that it is a mark of great intelligence (or maybe you just think that all your friends are doing it already), you think that to write really good English and score superb marks in your work you need to write sentences that sound very posh and clever, that go on for a long, long time and explain the things that you are trying to say with extremely knowledgeable-sounding words, like icorribgle, hefalitis, compoilia, or conrikable, which you hope the teacher will read, assuming your teacher can read, and say, 'Wow, John, that is an amazing piece of writing, you are such a bright lad producing that superbly long sentence,' however, the trouble is that if you thought that, which many of my students still do even at university, you would be incredibly, superbly, wonderfully, totally, and utterly wrong—in fact, the reverse is true.

> Long sentences produce confusion.
> Keep your sentences to 20 words or less (on average)—your writing (and grades) will improve.

If you want to write better English, write shorter sentences.

Most of us write sentences that are just way too long. Just like that one above that I put you through. And the problem is that if a sentence is long, it is more difficult to follow. You are more likely to repeat yourself. You are more likely to write a boring sentence. And, most importantly, the reader loses track completely of what it is that you are trying to say. In short, they are ineffective.

Useful Rule Number 3: Great Writing is Being Clear

> **Remember: being a good essay writer is not about having all sorts of imaginative adjectives and witty language.**
>
> **The goal of great writing is CLARITY.**
>
> **CLARITY is better than CLEVERNESS.**

Think to yourself: 'Will someone readily understand what it is that I am saying? Is my point clear? Does my evidence relate logically to what I am saying? Are my sentences flowing naturally one from the other?'

Don't bog your reader down with super-cleverly-smart phrases, or sickeningly-awfully-bad adjectives. Go for precise nouns. Quality verbs. Clear expression. When you do:

★   You will be more readily understood.
★   People will enjoy your writing.
★   You are less likely to make a mistake with your grammar.
★   Your grades will go up.

POLISHING
YOUR WORK
Techniques to Make Your Essay Shine

Improving Your Words is Part of the Journey

Improving your vocabulary is one of the steps to writing better essays. Great words alone don't make an A-grade essay—you need more than that—but in all the A-grade essays I have seen, the writer is showing that they are pushing themselves, and not being lazy by picking the first word that comes to mind.

Extending your word power even a bit will help you polish your essay writing and push your grade-scoring ability higher. Here are some good words to start using in your essays:

* demeaning
* persuasive
* contradiction
* justified
* compatible
* masterly
* enthralling
* dignified
* affluent
* vivid

* affronted
* contempt
* nationalism
* assuage
* demonstrated
* crucially
* banana (okay, I just threw that one in to see if you were still awake . . .)

The Essay in 3 Drafts

Polishing your essay is aided if you write it across 3 drafts. This does not mean that you have to rewrite your entire essay 3 times over. That is not necessary. However, each of the times that you 'draft' your essay, you look to improve particular aspects of your work. Here's how it works.

Draft 1

In draft 1 you plan your essay and write the first version of it in full, according to your plan. Include all your examples and evidence, and write your introduction and conclusion, based on the suggestions in this book. By the end of this process you have a completed essay. What you do not have is your BEST essay, which is why I recommend two further drafting techniques.

Draft 2

In draft 2 of your essay you check for several obvious errors and rewrite material where you see improvement can be achieved. In particular, look to improve your writing in the following areas:

1) Check that you have actually answered the question that was asked.
2) Check whether the evidence you have given is detailed enough.

Detailed evidence, written well, always gets more marks than superficial generalised comments.

Draft 1

Draft 2

Draft 3

3) Check to see if you have included all the material from your plan: are there any points where you need to put in additional information?
4) Check to see that you have stayed on topic. Are your paragraphs of similar lengths: are some over / under length?
5) Check to see that the point you make in each paragraph is clear AND that there is only ONE idea discussed per paragraph.

This completes your second draft.

Draft 3

Draft 3 is best completed after some time has elapsed since you undertook draft 2. Ideally, you should wait 24 hours before you come back to read your essay over one final time.

This time, as you undertake draft 3, you will read your essay with fresh eyes, and in so doing give yourself the very best opportunity to spot errors that you previously missed.

During draft 3 check for:

1) Grammatical mistakes.
2) Spelling errors.
3) Readability. Have you sufficient variety in your sentences? Are they interesting to read? Work to eliminate any difficult phrasing, or any particularly long sentences.

Final task

Before you complete draft 3, carry out this final task: read your essay out loud. It is too easy to miss errors in an essay when you sit in silence reading to yourself.

Speaking out loud what you have written is the BEST technique for adding final sparkle to your work. Your ear will hear how easy (or how difficult) it is for someone else to understand your essay.

The Empathetic Response

The majority of essays you have to write in school will be argument-based essays. As I have explained in this book, your teacher (or your exam marker) is wanting you to take a position on a topic and produce an evidence-based argument.

 Some examinations give you the choice to write an empathetic response: imitating the style of another author.

One other sort of writing that arises occasionally is the empathetic response. This a special kind of writing in English literature that doesn't occur frequently but I will explain it, as some of you may decide you would like to have a go at one.

Empathetic means in sympathy with—in the same style as—meaning you try and imitate the style of a writer to show your sensitivity to literature, and to demonstrate how polished your writing skills are. Because of this, an empathetic response is not an argument-based essay.

For example, if you had to write a paragraph from Shakespeare, and in your own words imitate his style of writing, you couldn't write:

(pointing to Juliet) 'Hey there, good-looking. Why don't you come down here from that balcony, so we can talk about going out together next Friday? I might even buy you a burger.'

While that might work in a modern drama class, it isn't going to cut it as Shakespeare. Try something like this instead:

(hand on heart) 'Juliet, my princess. Is that you my fairest I can discern from the window box afar? Thou art the loveliest of all the damsels I have seen, wondrous of form and beauty. Wouldst thou descend from your magnificent heights, and accompany me this Friday night to a banquet?'

Okay, so not quite Shakespearean, but you get the idea. Empathetic writing attempts to emulate the writing style of the author.

A Brief Guide to Empathetic Responses

Here are some things to look for if you have to write an empathetic response:

1) Attempt to mimic the voice of the author: the writing style, punctuation, diction, character development.
2) Observe how they start their sentences: do they use lots of verbs or adverbs to commence sentences?
3) Look at the sentence length generally: do they write long, or short, sentences?
4) Do they write in a particular tense?
5) Do they spend a lot of time describing things: characters, places, or feelings? If so, you need to do this also.

6) Is the language very formal, or informal?

7) Is there a lot of speech, or very little?

8) Does the author use letters between characters, or speeches, or notes to convey what characters think or say? You may need to imitate this also.

9) Do they spend much time describing actions?

10) Who is the narrator? What is their perspective: first person, or third person?

11) Does the character let you inside their feelings? Does the author relate their own feelings?

12) What is the pace of the book: do events happen quickly, or is a scene or moment drawn out at length?

All these style choices distinguish one writer from another, and are worth considering as you write your empathetic response.

On the Use of 'I'

Many students wonder: 'Can I use "I" in my essay? Can I say: "I feel that ..."?' Teachers can differ in their opinion on this issue, but as a whole, essays in English literature, especially essays discussing poetry, encourage the use of 'I' in the body of the essay as the subject is demanding a personal response to the material being discussed. A poetry essay, especially, is testing to see how you responded to the poem, and how it affected your feelings and emotions as a reader. If you answer such a question entirely formally, then you will miss out on some valuable marks. Be prepared to put some personal responses in your essay. For example, you might write in this sort of style:

> The dramatic imagery in stanza two, as the lion pounced on the defenceless gazelle, caused me almost to tremble. Immediately I sensed the vulnerability of the moment, and in the helpless gazelle, I saw the plight of the poor and the destitute in society.

If you feel uncomfortable using 'I' in your essay, try the phrase 'the reader' instead. This phrase can be quite effective, for like using 'I', the phrase 'the reader' signals that you are considering how the work of literature might be impacting on someone's emotional state. Here is how the above example might be rewritten using the phrase 'the reader':

> The dramatic imagery in stanza two, as the lion pounced on the defenceless gazelle, causes the reader almost to

tremble. Immediately you sense the vulnerability of the moment, and in the helpless gazelle, the reader feels the plight of the poor and the destitute in society.

- -

Essays in economics, history, geography, art history, classical studies, or media studies generally do not encourage the pervasive use of 'I' and can be adequately written using the third person. This means that you may use the following sorts of phrases in your essay to emphasise some of your points:

★ 'It is clear that . . .'
★ 'It appears that . . .'
★ 'The suggestion that . . .'
★ 'As this essay has argued . . .'
★ 'The point remains that . . .'
★ 'What seems obvious . . .'
★ 'What seems apparent was that . . .'
★ 'This essay will show . . .'
★ 'This essay suggests that . . .'
★ 'As this essay has demonstrated . . .'
★ 'This essay will examine the . . .'

Any of the above phrases suggest that you are taking a side and presenting an opinion, but you are doing so without bringing in the first person pronoun 'I'.

Staying on Topic

Do you ever feel when you are writing that you are beginning to stray off the topic? It can be an easy mistake to make, especially when you get captivated by a particular line of enquiry as you write and, before you know it, you end up using valuable words writing about ideas or issues that are not central to the question being asked.

Writing an **essay plan** is the best aid to help you stay on topic: **repeating useful phrases from the question** can also help.

One technique that can help you overcome such wandering is to use a key word or phrase from the question you have been asked and repeat this at opportune moments during your essay.

For example, say you were asked the question: How does author Joseph Heller use irony in the novel *Catch-22*? In this particular book, there are plentiful examples of irony, but to stay focused in your essay, you might use the word 'irony' in the opening sentence of some of your body paragraphs—or equally, in the closing sentence of a body paragraph, which is another useful place to drop in a word or phrase from the question.

Equally, you can use derivatives of a word in the question. So, taking the above example, I might use the following phrases when discussing an event in the book: 'It is ironic that . . .' or: 'In a deeply ironic moment . . .'.

A similar technique is to use synonyms of the word to add variety and still remain focused in your answer. For the above question, I might use words like 'paradox' or 'satirical'.

Repeating a key word or phrase from the question in the body of your essay not only says to the person reading your work that you are staying on topic, it forces YOU to stay on topic as you write. The key word or phrase from the question is a constant reminder to keep your examples and evidence on target and relevant.

Writing an Exam Essay

Writing an essay for an exam is just like the essay process written about in this book, with only TWO significant differences.

The **first major difference** is that you do not have much time, so you need to be condensed in your approach to planning your essay. You need to plan your exam essays: as to an examiner it is immediately obvious come exam time which students took even just a couple of minutes to sketch a quick plan, and which students wrote blindly to no plan, and often wandered off topic as a result. Write a plan for an exam essay and you will produce a more structured and focused essay.

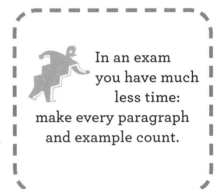

In an exam you have much less time: make every paragraph and example count.

The **second major difference** about an essay for an exam is that you want to advance as quickly as possible into writing the body of the essay. Consequently, practise writing 2-sentence introductions. To do this, write a **neutral** sentence opening the topic in a general sense, and then immediately write a sentence **explicitly saying** what the argument is in your essay, and the viewpoint you are proposing.

Then, begin to answer that in the very next paragraph. For exams, you want to rapidly begin notching up marks, and you win the most marks by what you compose in the body paragraphs. Long introductions do not win examination marks. Thoughtful, well-evidenced, interesting body paragraphs win marks.

How to Really Study

Study is not simply sitting down reading a book on your topic. That is passive, and unless you are swotting for a reading exam, you will not be showing up on exam day to read. You will have to show up on exam day and write an essay—or three.

The best exam practice is to rehearse what it is that you actually have to do in the exam. If you have to write an essay for your exam, practise writing essays on the topic in your course.

Study groups are also useful. Form a small group of three or four friends who are preparing for an examination and discuss how you would approach particular essay questions. Share your ideas and thoughts. Then, go away and write your practice essays. When your study group reconvenes, try reading your practice essays out loud to one another. It is a great way to sharpen your writing skills, and to discover new approaches to examination questions. Everyone in the group improves.

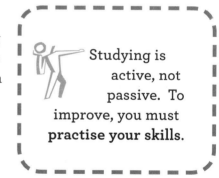

Studying is active, not passive. To improve, you must **practise your skills.**

Benefits of Rehearsing Your Essay Skills

★ As you write out your practice essays you will stumble on areas that you need to know more about—this is useful as it immediately identifies your weak areas. Stop, go find the information you need, then write it up in your essay. This way, essay writing is an active study tool as you plug the holes in your learning.

★ Writing essays to rehearse for exam day will increase your writing speed and stamina. This is a good thing. Some students just don't write enough in their exams. If you practise, your writing speed will increase and you also increase the likelihood of scoring a top mark.

Essay-Writing Checklist

If you have written your essay, and feel it is ready to hand in, do one final inspection using this handy checklist.

Tick the following:

- [ ] I have written a plan.
- [ ] In my introduction I have clearly stated my argument.
- [ ] I have got ONE main point per paragraph.
- [ ] The point of each paragraph is clear.
- [ ] I have used detailed examples to support each point.
- [ ] My paragraphs are the correct length—neither too short nor too long.
- [ ] My sentences are, on average, 20 words or less.
- [ ] I have used a variety of evidence in my essay paragraphs.
- [ ] I have only used quotes of 10 words or less.
- [ ] I have varied the styles of sentences in my essay.
- [ ] I have used good words to express myself.
- [ ] My conclusion states my main points and gives some thoughtful comments.
- [ ] I have proofread for spelling mistakes.
- [ ] I have read my essay with 'fresh eyes'—waiting 24 hours to check my writing.
- [ ] I have given my essay a title and written my name on it.

Time to Write

If you haven't tried writing your own essay yet, now is the time to start. Using the techniques described in this book:

★ Think about your question.

★ Plan your work.

★ Write your introduction, paying careful attention to stating your argument upfront.

★ Build the body of your essay using detailed evidence.

★ Show you can analyse and think about your question.

★ Think about your sentences and the ways you can improve your expression.

★ Round off with a strong conclusion—make a bold statement, deliver a thoughtful insight—tell the person reading your essay what the MOST important point you made was, and why.

★ Spend some time polishing and refining your work.

You Can Do It

I hope by now that you are thinking that writing this essay stuff is not as hard as you thought it was. And even if you never grow to LOVE essay writing, from reading this book and practising its techniques you will know enough about essay writing that when you do write, you will demonstrate a whole new level of skill and competency. And your grades will show it.

Now, go to it. Best wishes.

Dr Ian Hunter, Ph.D.